Women Today

Motherhood

by
Elizabeth Sirimarco

FRANKLIN PIERCE
COLLEGE LIBRARY
RINDGE, N.H. 03461

The Rourke Corporation, Inc.
Vero Beach, Florida 32964

To My Mother,
Thank You

Copyright 1991 by The Rourke Corporation, Inc.

All rights reserved. No part of this book may be reproduced or utilized in any form or by any means, electronic or mechanical, including photocopying, recording or by any information storage and retrieval system without permission in writing from the publisher.

The Rourke Corporation, Inc.
P.O. Box 3328, Vero Beach, FL 32964

Sirimarco, Elizabeth, 1966-
    Motherhood / by Elizabeth Sirimarco
        p. cm. —(Women today)
    Includes index.
    Summary: Looks at the ever-changing definition of motherhood and the variety of life styles and social situations of modern American mothers, including working mothers, single and divorced mothers, and feminist mothers.
    ISBN 0-86593-121-6
    1. Mothers—United States—Juvenile literature. 2. Motherhood—United States —Juvenile literature. [1. Mothers.] I. Title. II. Series: Women today (Vero Beach, Fla)
HQ759. S56   1991
306.874'3—dc20   91-11169
                                                                            CIP
                                                                             AC

CURR
HQ
759
S56
1991

Series Editor: Elizabeth Sirimarco
Editors: Gregory Lee, Marguerite Aronowitz
Book design and production: The Creative Spark, Capistrano Beach, California
Cover Photograph: Jon Feingersh/Tom Stack & Associates

Contents

1 *Mom In The '90s*

What image does the word mother conjure up in your mind? Does a mother stay home to raise her children? Does she have a job to help pay her family's bills, or is it because she wants to have interests and responsibilities outside the family? Does she have a high-powered career, while the father stays home to raise the children? Any of these can be true. Motherhood has no single job description. Some mothers are married, some are divorced. Some were never married. Some new mothers haven't reached age 20, others are over 40.

Every year, the typical American family becomes harder to define. Maybe you've seen some of the old television shows from the 1950s, like *Leave It To Beaver* or *Father Knows Best*. These portrayed idealized versions of American life, much like television shows created today. But they can still give you an idea about what it meant to be a "typical" mother four decades ago. For example, in the 1950s, most mothers did not work outside the home. They cleaned, cared for their children, cooked, sewed, and performed other domestic duties. If a child had to be disciplined or needed advice, it was customary to wait for father to come home from work: Father was head of the household—advisor, disciplinarian, and money-maker. Women did what they could to help their husbands and raise successful, well-behaved children.

In the late 1940s, after World War II, the United States was economically stable. The war was over, unemployment was low, and the nation was generally confident and upbeat. Husbands were earning enough so that wives could stay home and run the household. Since mom was at home and finances were in order, people had more babies. This period from 1946 to 1964 became known as the *baby boom* era because such a great increase in the birth rate occurred.

Then, in the 1960s, women began to question the status quo, or the typical and expected way that things are. Housewives became frustrated. They felt they were only able to live their lives through the successes and failures of their families. As a result of this dissatisfaction, *feminism* began to sweep the nation.

Feminism wasn't a new idea. There were women in medieval Europe who had questioned the treatment of their sex. In the late 18th century, Mary Wollstonecraft wrote an important essay about the rights of women. Her daughter, Mary Shelley, became the well-respected novelist who wrote *Frankenstein*. In the 19th century, women in both the United States and Great Britain worked hard to secure legal rights for women in marriage, education, and employment. From 1860 to 1920, the *suffragettes* worked in the United States to win the right for women to vote. Amendments to the Constitution allowing women equal rights were proposed as early as 1920.

But the 1960s feminist movement was different. It had a broader scope. Women wanted to achieve major changes in their way of life. They decided that the lifestyle of the 1950s was lacking, and they began to demand equality with men. The Women's Liberation movement, as it was called, caused major social change, particularly in the areas of family and career.

The Women's Movement

One of the most important goals of the late 20th century feminist was to achieve for women the right to satisfying and fulfilling careers. Oddly enough, the 20th century was one of the first times in history when a majority of women did not have to work. In the past, only wealthy married women had the luxury of staying home with their children. And unmarried women with money engaged in charitable activities or volunteer work so as not to disgrace their families. Women who needed to support themselves or supplement their husband's income worked in a great many capacities. They were farmers and seamstresses, teachers and bakers, weavers and ranchers. Some worked out of their home or on the family farm, while others worked away from home. And many times, in the case of women with children, this was in addition to their duties as mothers.

At the beginning of the 20th century, Americans adopted the idea of the *family wage*, which meant that married male workers were paid enough money to support their families. This, of course, meant that men were expected to earn more money than working women. But because most women were supported by their husbands, this was not a great concern. During the first half of the 20th century, many women worked—particularly during times of war. In World War II, for example, women worked because so many men were overseas, leaving critical jobs unfilled.

During the baby boom generation, most American women stayed home to take care of their families. During this era it was out of the ordinary—even a bit of a disgrace—for a married woman with children to work. It usually meant that her husband couldn't support his family or "control his wife." This attitude prevailed until the mid-1960s, when women began exploring and inventing new options.

In the 1970s, the *Equal Rights Amendment* (ERA) was proposed to Congress. Its most important goal was that "Equality of rights under the law shall not be denied or abridged by the United States or by any State on account of sex." Its purpose was to reduce economic and other forms of discrimination against women. Congress passed the ERA in 1972, but in order for it to become part of the Constitution, three quarters of the states would have had to ratify it by 1982, and this did not happen. While today equal rights for women are not guaranteed by the Constitution, there are laws that protect women against discrimination in the workplace and elsewhere.

Even without the ERA, the 1970s and early 1980s

Women around the country fought for the Equal Rights Amendment in the 1970s and '80s. Although it did not become law, women began to pursue careers in male-dominated professions.

saw millions of American women filing into the work force. And they weren't satisfied to just pursue "traditional" female careers like teaching, nursing, or secretarial work. They wanted to be lawyers, businesswomen, and doctors. They were staying single longer to pursue their careers and experience their new-found independence. In three decades the average age for a woman's first marriage increased by four years.

Suddenly it was no longer acceptable to stay home and raise children. Says one author, "Families were seen as the problem, not the solution." There was a rapid decline in the American birth rate—so much so that it has been called the baby bust era. This is the opposite of the baby boom era. Some women even chose not to have families at all. Many housewives envied the single, childless women whose lives seemed so glamorous. Their own lives seemed less important, and motherhood quickly lost its esteem.

By the early 1970s, however, many career women decided that they were missing out—they wanted children like their counterparts who had chosen to stay home. Magazines began talking about the goal to "have it all"—a satisfying career and a happy family with two or three children.

Many people think we are currently in another baby boom. In 1987, the birth rate was higher than it had been in any year since 1964. Married couples increased by three percent during the 1980s. Still, it hasn't approached the rate of the post-war era. This is in part because women are waiting until they are older to have children. Women over age 30 giving birth for the first time have more than quadrupled since 1970. Women who are older when they become pregnant have fewer children, however, so their families tend to be smaller. Polls indicate that young women who plan to become mothers usually want two, possibly three children. The average number of children per family in the United States is 1.16. During the boom years—1946 to 1964—families of four or six children were not unusual.

Even if today's birth rate isn't exactly a boom, there continues to be an increased interest in child bearing. Women across the United States are setting their sights on families. They hope to be the generation that strikes a balance between career and family. They want good careers and children, and they don't want their children to be raised by strangers. Says one young career woman, "I could have all the success in the world, but if I wasn't lucky enough to have a family to share it with, it wouldn't mean a thing."

Maybe the next generation of mothers will have more options than those of today. While women chose to work in the 1970s and early 1980s, many mothers *have* to work in the 1990s. Families find it difficult to survive on just one income. Women who make the choice to stay home often do so knowing it will mean serious financial difficulties. Working mothers juggle busy careers and child-rearing; most find it isn't easy to "have it all." The many women who choose to stay home with their children spend equally tiring, often thankless days caring for home and family. It's difficult to make a family work today. Women have more opportunities and choices, but they aren't easy ones.

The "Mommy Wars"

An interesting phenomenon of the 1990s is the *Mommy Wars*, a term coined by *Newsweek* magazine. To the at-home mother, her working counterpart appears to be a cold, selfish woman who works not to help support her family, but to afford luxury items or achieve success. Even though she has children, she won't commit to them on a full-time basis. To the working mother, the woman who stays home to raise her children appears to be lucky, maybe even a little lazy. She couldn't possibly have anything to keep her busy at home all day. No doubt she watches soap operas, works out at fitness clubs and goes shopping with other non-working mothers.

About 84 percent of at-home mothers think staying home makes them better mothers; 61 percent of them say they miss the money they would earn if they worked. Forty-three percent of working moms say they make better mothers; 67 percent of them say they miss their children while at work. Working mothers worry that their children will love the babysitter more than mom. At-home mothers worry that they won't be as interesting to their children or to other adults as working women. Working mothers worry that the day-care centers won't take good care of their children—or worse, that they will neglect or abuse them. At-home mothers worry that they perpetuate the idea that women belong at home, and that their children won't respect them when they grow up.

Motherhood is a time-consuming and rewarding job—for both women who choose to stay at home and those who pursue a career.

In 1960, only 19 percent of women with children under the age of six were in the labor force. Today 56 percent of them have jobs outside the home. Working mothers, like those who stay at home, want to be certain they've made the right choice. To defend their decision, they may criticize mothers who have chosen a different route. Those who stay at home are dull or not smart enough to get "a real job," say some working mothers. Mothers who work can't raise responsible, well-adjusted children because they are insensitive, masculine, uncaring beings, say the at-home moms. Writer Anita Shreve notes that "there exists in America today a deep and sharp division" between the two kinds of mothers. "And no small cause of that split is that one group feels exploited and/or dismissed by the other."

Rather than argue about the differences between them, mothers of all kinds would be wise to focus instead on what they have in common. For example, mothers—both working and at-home—specify their children's well-being as top priority. Both work very hard and make sacrifices to do what they think is best for their families. Researcher Lisa C. Harris interviewed both types of mothers and found that working moms often spent as much quality time with their children as their nonworking counterparts because they give up the time they would otherwise spend on personal interests. "My husband and I did our own random survey," says Harris, "of children whom we admired for a variety of different characteristics. When we looked at their family backgrounds, we realized that as many came from households where mother worked outside the home as from households where the mother was a homemaker."

The best mothers are the ones who love their children and who are happy with their lives, whichever path they've chosen. Women who are depressed about their roles tend to have unhappy children. What the women's movement has done is allowed women to accomplish their goals before they have children. Women who have developed a strong sense of independence and identity before they have children have more to offer their children. They are generally more concerned with the children than themselves because they have already achieved many of their dreams and goals. Carol Bloom, a psychotherapist, remarks that women who have babies before they have lived their own lives may feel some resentment later in life. "A woman could be subject to some of the same feelings women had 30 or 40 years ago, the sense of not really having lived."

Women who work because they want to are good mothers. Women who work special hours or make careful, complex arrangements to spend as much time with their children as possible are good mothers.

Women who put a successful career on hold to spend a few years with the children they love are good mothers. Many working mothers say they'd stay home at least part time if they could afford it; many at-home mothers say they would work if they could find part-time jobs with flexible hours or acceptable child care. There still aren't a lot of options for mothers, even though the feminist movement's major goal was to give women more choices. Neither working nor staying home is the right or wrong choice. But hopefully, the future will give families more options so mothers *and* fathers can spend more time with their children.

2 *The Working Mother*

Karen Glass wakes every weekday morning at 5:30. She goes to the kitchen to start a pot of coffee for herself and her husband, then takes a quick shower. She pulls on her robe, hair still dripping wet, then starts preparing breakfast. Usually this means cold cereal for her five-year-old son Jeremy and baby food for her year-old daughter, Micah. It's a little after six o'clock when she wakes the children and her husband, Tom, who prepares to go to work.

After Karen feeds the children, she gets them dressed for school and the day-care center. Tom eats his own breakfast quickly so he can watch the kids while she dresses for work. By seven o'clock, everyone is ready to leave. First Karen drops Tom off at the train station so he can began his commute into New York City, about an hour's trip. Then she drives on to Jeremy's kindergarten, a private school that has a day-long class. Micah goes to a day-care center close to Karen's office, a 30-minute drive from home. Karen often comments how lucky she feels to have this extra time with her daughter in the morning.

After all the running around, Karen gets to work at eight o'clock, then works until five. Sometimes she stops at the grocery store to pick up food for dinner. She picks up her family in reverse order of the morning drop-off ritual. They get home at six o'clock, and Karen immediately starts dinner. After dinner, the family spends time together. Jeremy often needs help with his new reading skills. Sometimes they read a story together, watch television, or play a game while Micah sits on Karen's lap. At eight o'clock, Karen gives both children a bath, then puts them to bed. Then it's time to do the dishes and get any other needed housework done before she goes to bed. Tom helps, too, but he often has extra work he's had to bring home. Saturdays are devoted almost exclusively to housework. Sundays are "family days": They go to the zoo, to a movie, or to a friend or relative's house for dinner.

Karen's life is typical of many working mothers. She has little time to pursue personal interests, little time to spend with her children, and little time to spend alone with her husband.

Women with children are often discriminated against in subtle ways on the job. The *mommy track* is a term used to describe the faltering careers of many working mothers. They've had to take off a few weeks during and after pregnancy, so employers claim they aren't truly devoted to their jobs. Once they have children, they are able to devote less time to their careers in order to care for their children. They might miss work to care for a sick child, so other "more motivated" employees get promotions quicker and more easily. Women wonder why a man's career is never changed when his family decides to have a baby. That's one thing the women's movement has not changed. Finding a way to raise children and have productive careers is one of the most challenging aspects of motherhood in the 1990s.

Maternity Leave

The United States is the only industrialized nation besides South Africa to have no nationally guaranteed *maternity leave*, or a leave of absence taken by a woman when she has a child. European families enjoy excellent national leave policies. The Swedish government, for example, provides parents with 90 percent of the mother's salary while she stays at home with the baby for the first nine months after birth. Under President Gorbachev, the Soviet Union offers women nine months of paid maternity leave, with the option of taking another nine months leave without pay. Because the Soviet Union has an ongoing labor shortage, they want to do everything they can to encourage women to return to the work force. New mothers are assured of having their jobs when they return. In addition, families are encouraged to have children because of the decline

Coordinating career and home can take all the time and energy a woman has, leaving her feeling stressed due to an overwhelming work load.

in the Soviet birth rate, so maternity leaves suit a dual purpose.

In 1990, Congress tried to pass a law that would guarantee working mothers six weeks of unpaid leave after having a baby. President Bush vetoed the bill, mostly because of strong lobbying by business groups. It can be difficult and costly for companies, particularly smaller ones, to hold jobs for absent employees over a long period of time. The loss of one employee can greatly increase the work load of others.

Parental leave legislation has been introduced in Congress every year since 1985. Parental leave is the same as maternity leave, only it would allow either the mother or father to care for a newborn or adopted child. It also would allow a parent to stay home from work to care for a sick child. Some companies in the United States do offer parental leave, even though they are not required to do so by law. These leaves can last from a few days to more than a year, but are almost always unpaid. An employee on parental leave is guaranteed the same or a similar job when he or she returns to work, with no loss of benefits (like health insurance or retirement pensions) or seniority. It is much easier for a large company to offer its employees parental leaves than a small one. In fact, many small companies would be forced to eliminate other benefits to make room for mandatory parental leave. This would be unfair to the employees who do not take advantage of parental leave.

The Pregnancy Discrimination Act of 1978 is the only federal law that accommodates the needs of working mothers. This act prohibits discrimination (such as loss of job) because of pregnancy. It does not, however, require employers to provide a specific number of weeks for maternity leave. Employers typically treat pregnancy in much the same way as they treat a short-term illness or disability. This means a woman may be considered medically disabled for a week or two before her delivery date and for six to eight weeks afterward. Often, though, companies do not pay even disabled employees for more than five "sick days" a year.

In 1977 a woman named Nora Satty took a leave of absence because of pregnancy, but found that her job was not waiting for her when she returned to work. Her company's policy guaranteed employees their jobs if they took a leave of absence for disability or disease, but did not offer the same rights to pregnant women. In a court case, it was found that Satty's employer was discriminating against her by imposing a burden on women that was not imposed on men.

If a company's policy does not guarantee a person's job after an extended leave of absence for any kind of disability, then pregnant women will be treated no differently. This is why so many people want maternity leave to be a right guaranteed by federal law. It is becoming harder and harder for companies around the country to ignore the parental leave issue, because 51 percent of women with children under age two are in the work force—20 percent more than in 1977. "We can't make such a drastic change without having the workplace accommodate it," says Paul Rupert, associate director of New Ways To Work, an organization that helps parents face the challenge of working and raising children.

Day Care

One dilemma that all working mothers share is finding safe, reliable, and affordable care for their children. The costs of day care can be so high that families find it actually doesn't help the total family income for both parents to work. When the cost of day care, commuting, clothing for work, additional federal and state taxes, and other work-related expenses are added up, they sometimes reach dollar amounts so high that it equals what the second income brings in. One Colorado mother found that after all expenses were considered, she was only earning 35 cents an hour— about four dollars an hour less than minimum wage.

There are many different kinds of day care. Some women are fortunate enough to have a relative— perhaps a mother or sister—who can take care of the children during the day. These women are usually happy that their child is receiving the best care anyone but themselves could give, and it is usually the most affordable. Another form of child care is the *au pair*. These are young women from foreign countries, usually just out of high school, who want to come to the United States. In exchange for room, board, and a small salary (usually about $5,000 a year), *au pairs* will provide live-in child care and light housework for their employers. The downside of this kind of child care is that the young women are generally only hired for one year, so the search for a new *au pair* becomes a yearly problem.

Residents started this day-care center in the Kenilworth-Parkside housing project in Washington, D.C.

In addition, if the young woman becomes homesick or unhappy with her situation, she may leave at any time.

Another live-in form of day care is the *nanny*. These professionally trained women are usually older than *au pairs*. Consequently, they are much more expensive—$14,000 to $19,000 a year, plus room and board. Other choices include a daily babysitter who will come to a family's home to care for children. In 1990, the standard rate for this type of care was about $7 an hour, adding up to about $17,500 each year. Children can also be cared for by day-care mothers, who take children into their homes for $3.50 an hour per child. For one-child families, this is often an excellent option. But with two or three children, the price reaches from $14,000 to $21,000 a year.

Day-care Centers

Day-care centers are similar to preschools. They are

places where children from infancy to school age are cared for from the time their parent drops them off in the morning until they go home at night. Many families choose these centers as day care for their children but it, too, is expensive. Licensed day-care centers can cost anywhere from $5,000 to $8,000 per child each year. In New York, the average family spends 19 percent of its annual income on child care.

Many day-care centers are well-run and safe for children. Quite a few are operated in neighborhood churches and synagogues. Some are part of progressive teaching programs like the Montessori school system. In recent years, however, stories of neglect and abuse in child care centers have appeared in the media. For example, a man in California was tried for sexually abusing children at his day-care center. A New York day-care center was accused of forcing children to drink lemon juice as punishment. When parents hear these horrible stories in the news, they cannot help but worry about their own child's day-care situation.

Legislation

In 1987, a bill called the Act for Better Child Care Services (known as the ABC bill) was introduced in Congress. At first glance, it looked like a life-saver for working mothers. It would have provided federal assistance for parents who earned up to $37,000 and helped fund education programs at day-care centers to give children a head start. It would demand specific training for all center employees and establish national standards for the regulation of day care in centers and day-care homes, hoping to protect children from abuse and neglect. ABC promised to make child care safer and more affordable for everyone.

The ABC bill died in 1988, but many parents and day-care specialists thought it would have been insufficient anyway. One reason is that even with a budget of $2.5 billion, ABC would have only amounted to aid of about $120 per year per child—about one or two weeks' worth of day care at best. Estimates were that to truly fulfill the promises of ABC, the actual budget would have to be $75 to $100 billion. It also would have taken choices away from parents about where they could seek care. Government-regulated day care could not support centers with church affiliations because of Constitutional laws about the separation of church and state. As much as 90 percent of current day-care arrangements—including unlicensed day care, care by relatives, and church-run centers—would be barred from receiving aid at all. Only centers that followed the procedures outlined by the state would receive assistance.

The government must offer some sort of aid to families who need day care, but so far a successful, carefully planned bill has not been presented to Congress. Today, only a small tax deduction helps deflect the cost of child care. While ABC was not the answer, the government must continue to seek ways of helping households that need two incomes to survive.

New Ways To Work

Some families have chosen to get creative with their work schedules in order to meet the demands of the household budget, the family, and the work force. Reduced or restructured work schedules often mean that one parent can be with the child all or part of the day. It reduces the cost of day care and also means the parent has the pleasure and security of raising a child.

New Ways To Work (NWTW), a San Francisco-based organization, works to help parents and other individuals, including the elderly and the handicapped, reshape a career to their needs. NWTW suggests a number of ways that parents can schedule work to give them more time for their family:

• **Flextime:** Work schedules that permit flexible starting and quitting times within limits set by management. Sometimes a husband and wife can arrange their schedules so one of them is almost always at home.

• **Compressed Work Week:** A work week (usually 40 hours long) compressed into less than five days. Maybe parents work four 10-hour days, instead of five 8-hour days. The mother can take one day off a week, the father takes another, leaving only three days a week needing child care.

• **Telecommuting:** Employees work off-site while linked to the office electronically. Computers and fax machines make it easier for individuals to work at home.

• **Part-Time Employment:** Employment for less than 40 hours a week that includes job security and other rights and benefits that are often only available to full-time employees.

• **Job Sharing:** A form of part-time work in which two people voluntarily share the responsibilities of one full time position. Each gets half the benefits and salary.

• **Reduced Time:** Allowing full-time employees to reduce work hours for a specified period of time with a corresponding reduction of pay. Parents can work part-time when family life makes it necessary.

• **Leaves of Absence:** Authorized periods of time away from work without loss of employment rights. May be paid or unpaid.

While it is still relatively unusual, some corporations are establishing on-site day-care centers. Campbell Soup Co., for example, opened a center at its facility in 1983. In 1990, the company-sponsored center took care of 125 children each day. They also offer leaves of absence up to six months, job sharing, flexible hours, and part-time work. The company has found that keeping its employees happy is good business practice. One dedicated employee who has sent three sons to Campbell's day-care center says, "I will give my all for this company. Campbell has helped me turn my family around." AT&T offers employees one year of unpaid

Campbell Soup's corporate day care program in Camden, New Jersey, makes life a little easier for the company's employees.

leave to care for infants or ill dependents. IBM offers its employees up to three years of unpaid leave with full benefits to raise children.

While not all companies are as generous as these, many are willing to work with valued employees. One study recently found that only 15 percent of expectant mothers were offered parental leave, but another eight percent took the initiative to arrange their own. Valued employees often have good luck negotiating for their special needs. In the future, an increased number of on-the-job day-care facilities, longer paid maternity leaves, and more opportunities for flexible work schedules will make the choice to work outside the home easier. These benefits, along with better national policies, will lessen the load for future working mothers.

Help From Dad

One thing women wanted the feminist movement to achieve was an equal share of responsibilities in the house. Women today expect more help from their husbands; if they earn half the family's income, they should only perform half of the household duties. Fathers on television and in the movies are usually shown as caring and involved in parenting; husbands are helpful and sensitive. But have men really changed that much in the last 30 years?

According to a recent poll of American mothers from 18 to 80, only one in every 10 women feels that she shares household and child-rearing responsibilities equally with her husband. Full-time homemakers expect their husbands to do less in the house, but working mothers feel frustrated by having to perform two full-time jobs. As one mother said, "He is only supportive of my interests and activities as long as I do all the housework, child rearing, and work a 40-hour week." "I think my most frustrating time is when I have cooked dinner and have had to leave for a PTA meeting," said another. "When I come home, I find all the dishes and food still on the table for me to clean up."

Some mothers feel their husbands simply don't realize how hard they work. But for the women who receive the help they need or want from their husbands, motherhood is a much more pleasant job.

Mr. Mom

In some households, the husband does a great deal of the housework, as well as the parenting. This is a new form of child care that people wouldn't have dreamed of even 20 years ago. Today, in an ever-increasing number of households, fathers are staying home to raise their children while their wives "bring home the bacon."

Kate Mitchell is a Los Angeles executive who started a small, successful advertising company nine years ago.

A father walks his four-year-old son to school. Men who share the
responsibilities of family life are becoming more common, but most
women still feel they perform the lion's share of work at home.

She leaves home at eight o'clock each morning. Waving goodbye to daughter Amber and husband Mike, she drives to her office where she employs three other people.

"I've spent the last nine years getting customers. Since I run the business, I couldn't take a maternity leave. My clients would have taken their business somewhere else," says Kate.

Kate brought Amber to the studio for the first six weeks so she could breast feed. "But it was impossible. I couldn't get work done. Mike is an artist, but he hasn't had much luck selling his work yet. We always knew he'd be the one to care for a child. He's more patient. It was easier for him to adjust."

After two years, neither Kate nor Mike have any complaints about their unusual arrangement. "I know that people say a lot of things about it," says Mike. "Some men probably think I'm a wimp, and I've actually had women accuse me of being too lazy to support my family. It's funny. Sometimes women can be more sexist than men!"

Kate laughs and adds, "People wonder what kind of mother I could possibly be. But we're happy. And Amber is being raised by a parent. That's what matters."

In a *Time* magazine poll, 48 percent of American males between age 18 and 24 said they would be interested in staying home to care for their children if they had the opportunity. The next generation of parents may be luckier than those of today. Perhaps by then two-career families won't have to struggle so hard to stay afloat. When American government and industry work to assist the needs of their employees, it's possible that day-care dilemmas will be a thing of the past.

3 Mother At Home

T he feminist movement made it easier for women to set goals—and to reach them. Sallie Dashiell's life is different than it would have been had she been born 20 years earlier. Her story is one of success, and in the simplest terms, she seems to represent what the women's movement struggled to achieve. She has an advanced education. After acquiring a master's degree in Speech Pathology, she worked with mentally and physically handicapped adolescents in a Southern California school district for 12 years. In addition, she owned and managed two homes for severely handicapped individuals who could not live with their families. She worked long hours, but her career was satisfying, and she was well-respected.

Until Sallie was 35, her career took precedence over marriage and family. Like many women in the late 1970s and early '80s, she waited until she achieved her goals before starting a family. When she married her husband Paul in 1987, she chose to keep her own name. Within a year, they had their first child, Sarah.

At first Sallie intended to go back to work full time. When her daughter was three months old, she began working for the school district again. "It was impossible—the worst five months of my life. I was still managing the group homes, and the days just weren't long enough. Although I loved my work with the school district, I realized I didn't want to be distracted from my new job—taking care of Sarah," says Sallie. Soon after, she became a full-time mother. The school district offered Sallie two years of unpaid leave, and she took it.

When Sarah was two, Sallie had her second child, Lillie. She decided it was time to give up the group homes, and they were sold shortly before Lillie was born. Soon after, the school district contacted her, asking if she had any intention of coming back to work. "They felt I was keeping someone else out of a job, and they wanted me in or out of the position. I understood

Many women have chosen to stay home with their children simply because they enjoy being with them.

their situation, but after giving them my time for 12 years, it seemed they weren't as supportive as they could have been. No one seemed to think I was making a wise decision." She began consulting, helping schools and homes for the handicapped set up communication programs for their clients, but she tried to keep the hours at a minimum. "I usually take on consulting jobs that I can do in the evenings or on weekends when Paul is home with Sarah and Lillie."

Sallie loves staying at home with her children. She continues to do her consulting when there's time, but she hasn't any immediate plans to go back to work full time. "I catch myself thinking that the work I'm doing now isn't as significant as what I used to do, but I keep reminding myself that it is. I love what I'm doing. And it is a job. You just don't get paid for it. And unfortunately, you really don't get any recognition for as hard as you work. When you do, it's from other women who are going through the same things you are."

Sallie is an at-home mother. Women who stay home often give up successful careers to be with their children. Many strongly supported the women's movement; many consider themselves feminists. "There's a misconception that stay-at-home mothers have temporarily checked out of life to raise their children," says Christine Donovan, co-publisher of a newsletter for at-home mothers. "The truth is, today's at-home mother is home with her kids because she wants to be. It's a conscious choice made by many intelligent, vibrant women."

Choosing To Stay Home

In the 1950s, a woman was supported in her decision to stay home with her children. In fact, she was expected to do so. Working mothers were criticized for leaving their children in someone else's care. Today mothers who stay at home feel they are the ones receiving the criticism. "Sometimes working mothers make you feel as though you're trying to destroy everything the feminist movement has achieved," said one mother of two. "Sometimes they just make you feel stupid. But I have a college education. And I gave up a successful career because I wanted to take care of my children. I never thought of doing it another way."

As Sallie Dashiell suggested, even mothers themselves are not always convinced that staying home to care for children is a full-time and worthwhile job that a bright, motivated person would take on. Part of the problem is simply that at-home mothers are not paid for what they do. In a society where high salaries and status careers are the gauges of personal success, motherhood just doesn't seem to be as important.

Many at-home mothers became frustrated in their

Women who stay home do not spend their days watching television or shopping with friends. Their days can be difficult and busy.

careers. They hit the "glass ceiling," a place in a woman's career when she can no longer be promoted to a higher level because of prejudice and discrimination. Although there are laws protecting women from this kind of situation, it can be very difficult to prove you are being discriminated against. Women have grown tired of fighting for success and good child care. And they see how little government and business leaders are willing to do for them. For women who can afford it, staying home seems to be the only way to win.

But the women's movement has damaged the prestige of the at-home mom. Students at Wellesley College objected to inviting Barbara Bush to speak at their graduation because they believed that as an at-home mother, she didn't provide a suitable role model for young women leaving college. Women around the country were critical of television newswoman Connie Chung's decision to cut back on her highly successful work for motherhood.

Almost half of American mothers with children under the age of six stay home with their children. Maybe the at-home mother is lucky to have a spouse who can easily support a family with only a single income. Maybe a husband and wife have agreed to sacrifice so she can stay home. But even after three decades of change, American women still think it is important to care for their children. In fact, a poll of younger women who have not yet become mothers indicates that 66 percent of them would be interested in staying home with their children. "The whole women's movement is pushing the career women," says one college student, "and making light of being a homemaker." Clearly, the feminist movement has not discouraged women from doing what they think is best for their child.

Leslie Garris has worked as a writer out of her home since her children were born. But after years of struggling to be a mother and meet journalistic deadlines, she's decided to devote herself to full-time motherhood. "If I were unlucky enough to have an office job—and lucky enough to be financially able to leave it—I'd be quitting. As it is, I have some options. I can eliminate deadlines and still be a writer. Instead of doing journalism, I can finish the novel I've been working on." Mothers who stay at home have skills, aspirations and talents like those who work. They simply have different priorities.

About 49 percent of mothers stay home with their children who are one year old or younger. But when the children are six years or older, only 26 percent remain home. Quite a few mothers go back to work once their children are in school. After six years away from work, however, they usually have difficulty getting back into a good career. Similarly, women who have had children at a young age and never worked have a difficult time obtaining job skills if they decide to work later. Unfortunately, the business community does little to help women who have stayed home come back to the workplace.

A New Life

If a working woman decides to stay home after having a child, she and her husband will both have to be prepared for changes in their relationship. Of course, there is less money, but that is only one of the problems.

A woman might feel she is "less equal" because she no longer contributes to the household income. If her husband resents being the sole breadwinner in the family, negative feelings can develop. If both individuals haven't agreed on the arrangement and talked about what they expected their new lives to be like, misunderstandings can arise. Until the birth of the first child, husbands and wives often have separate bank accounts. Each might spend their money independently. Suddenly, when the wife stops working, she has to ask her husband for money. She has lost her financial independence.

Husbands and wives must determine each other's value by what they contribute to the family and the home. One of the biggest problems can be when the husband doesn't feel motherhood is an important or difficult experience. One thing many women feel has not changed after the women's movement is that women are still the ones who must compromise and sacrifice when children are born. "I loved my job, " says Lena Andrews, "and I intend to work again someday. I knew when I married my husband that he would never consider staying home to take care of the kids. Very few men would. But we both felt it was important that I did. So I put a successful and exciting career on hold because I love my two sons. But my husband's life seems to have gone on without any interruption or change."

Women who choose to stay home have a special commitment to their families. It can be difficult to abandon a career, even temporarily. But many American women think that family is even more important than career goals. They are willing, like mothers who work full-time, to make the sacrifices that motherhood demands.

4 *Single Mothers*

n the last 15 years, the number of families led by single parents has leaped by 230 percent in the United States. Almost all of these single parents are female. One family in four is headed by a woman, and that number is steadily increasing. Divorce is one reason. Others have *chosen* to have a child without a husband. Still others have been widowed. Some mothers have never been married. About 60 percent of American children are likely to spend part of their childhood or adolescence in a family with just one parent—usually their mother.

For a long time the single-parent family was unusual. They were different than other families, and people tended to treat them as such. Members of the "perfect" nuclear family looked at single-parent families with both respect and relief. They believed it was admirable that women could support their children financially and emotionally by themselves, but "better them than us." But by 1990, there were 9.7 million single parents in the nation. Nearly all of these single parents are mothers. And only 26 percent of the nation's 93.3 million households are composed of a married couple with children younger than 18. In 1990, the nuclear family had declined in number by five percent since the 1980s. Today single parents aren't so different anymore. When one-quarter of the population is part of a single-parent family, they are no longer a minority.

Divorce is the legal recognition that a marriage has ended. One or both partners has no desire to continue in the relationship. In 1989 an estimated 1.16 million divorces were granted in the United States. While this number had dropped slightly from the year before, it was still alarming. In 1960 the divorce rate was 2.2 percent. In 1980 it jumped to 5.2 percent.

Divorce is not a new idea. In ancient Jewish law, for example, a wife did not have the right to divorce her husband, but she did have the right to remarry if her husband divorced her. In the Roman Empire, couples

These single mothers share a house to help lower the cost of living.

simply began to live together in recognized, permanent households without any legality or marriage ceremony. Either the husband or wife could end the marriage simple by formally expressing his or her wish to do so.

In the United States, early American settlers had varied ideas about divorce. Catholics believed that marriage was sacred and there could be no divorce. Protestants believed that marriage and divorce were not just religious matters and that civil authorities could dissolve a marriage.

Divorce has never been illegal in any state, but until recently it was socially discouraged. A couple could not dissolve their marriage simply because they weren't getting along. A serious reason, like adultery, cruelty, desertion, or insanity was necessary for a couple to divorce in most states. The 20th century brought about the notion of the family wage, so few women could support themselves after a divorce. Men were generally required to pay *alimony* to support their wives. Because children were usually put in the custody of the mother, fathers also paid *child support* after a divorce. As the United States became increasingly urban, however, divorce became more common. By the late 1960s, "no-fault" divorce became common. Couples could separate because of "irreconcilable differences" instead of placing serious blame on one another. But no-fault divorce often meant that men were no longer required to pay alimony.

The women's movement greatly increased the divorce rate because for the first time in history, women around the world felt they could survive on their own. Divorce became a means of establishing one's independence. Unfortunately, it often had disastrous results for women who had no training to find an adequate job and no means of locating reliable, affordable child care.

Today most fathers are still required to pay child support. Unfortunately, divorced fathers often ignore child support obligations. Nicholas Zill, Ph.D., who researches a number of topics regarding children and the effects of divorce, notes, "What happens in most divorces is that the child goes to live with the mother, and then within a few years the father stops paying child support, stops maintaining contact with the family, and perhaps sets up another household." Today only slightly more than one-half of America's single mothers receive the child support they are entitled to.

Even when mothers do receive monthly child support payments, it seldom meets all the unexpected expenses. "When I first learned what my children would receive each month," says one mother of three, "I thought it would be enough to get by. But child support settlements never take into consideration all the things that you might need. My oldest son plays basketball and wants an expensive pair of sneakers. My daughter wants ballet lessons. Child support doesn't take these luxuries into consideration. And every month, some little accident happens. Maybe the car needs new brakes. Maybe the water heater breaks down. There's never enough money. And the household is entirely my responsibility."

A recent survey showed that 76 percent of adolescent children in mother-only homes are generally very satisfied with their families. Many children are actually happier when their parents divorce because they no longer live in a quarrelsome household. In addition these children often gain independence by observing their mothers struggling and succeeding in the world. They begin to view women as strong and competent because they have watched their mothers succeed. Although it may be ideal to have a happy home with both a mother and father in residence, there are many successful families led by mothers who have made the commitment to raise happy children without their husbands.

Single Mothers and Poverty

Many single mothers barely scrape by, working long hours and collecting whatever child support they can. But there are also women around the country who have it much worse. Some of these women were raised in poverty while others were raised in middle-class suburban homes. Some were never married, or were married and the husband is no longer a source of financial support. Many of these women are minorities, but many white women also share this predicament.

Nearly 80 percent of Americans living below the poverty line are women and dependent children. One welfare program, Aid to Families with Dependent Children (AFDC), provides financial support to these women and children. For women with one or more children, it can be very difficult to meet family expenses. Often these women have been abandoned by the children's father. Other times, he may simply neglect his child support obligations. In other instances, the woman was never married and the father has no legal obligation to help support the child. Many people accuse these women of being lazy or unwilling to work full-time jobs to support their family. In reality, they are often unable to find work that pays enough to meet their expenses. In addition, the expense of and difficulty locating reliable child care can make it impossible for these women to emerge in the work force. They are caught in an endless cycle of poverty.

Some women become so concerned about the well-being of their children that they give up custody of their children to the father. It is still unusual for the father to keep the children after a divorce, but sometimes both parents agree it is necessary. If the woman can get a job to support herself, she can have visitation rights, and the children will be able to continue their lives with the least amount of disruption.

AFDC recipients come from all walks of life—they are not only black women or Hispanics. Many are white women who had a child very early in life and then struggled with single motherhood. Many have been homemakers for so long that they no longer have the skills to get good jobs. Many are among the ever-increasing number of women from all backgrounds who become pregnant before they are married and receive no support from the child's father. Most women on welfare simply cannot join the work force because they do not have sufficient job skills to support their family. Says Congresswoman Pat Schroeder of Colorado, "…there are an incredible number of women who are one man away from poverty and don't know it."

The amount of money AFDC recipients receive

Many single mothers don't have the training necessary to find a good job. It can be difficult to learn a new profession and manage a family at the same time.

varies from state to state, but it is usually never enough money. In California, for example, AFDC checks amount to about $8,400 each year for a mother and two children. Since rent takes up about one-third of a family's monthly income, that only leaves about $450 for food, heat, clothing, transportation, water and all other expenses for the month. That isn't a lot of money for three people to live on.

Yet many people want AFDC payments to be reduced. Recently, Governor Pete Wilson of California had to cut the state budget. Welfare was one of the first programs he considered. In 1991, Wilson proposed a $225-million cut in the AFDC budget, meaning the monthly stipend would drop from $694 to $633. Wilson said, "I am convinced [AFDC recipients] will be able to pay the rent, but they will have less for a six-pack of beer. I don't begrudge them a six-pack, but I don't think it is an urgent necessity....I am not convinced that people who are not capable of earning [a living] are best left with discretion to spend."

There are women on welfare who abuse government aid, but many fight a daily struggle to raise their children in acceptable housing. They fight to feed and clothe their children. And too many children live in neighborhoods where they can become victims of drug-related violence.

Many politicians forget that single women with children who want to work must not only find a job that pays their bills, but one that will pay the additional cost of day care. For every woman who spends government aid unwisely, there are many more who use it to support their families in the only way they can. Budget cuts don't just deprive mothers of a six-pack of beer; they may deprive a child of new shoes when he outgrows his last pair. Or a nutritious dinner. Or a new coat to keep warm in cold winter months.

JOBS

In 1988, the Family Support Act was passed. Before that time, only AFDC cash assistance was available to needy mothers. Today, the Family Support Act helps these women learn to support themselves. Under this act, the Job Opportunities and Basic Skills (JOBS) program helps welfare recipients become employed and self-sufficient, and provides support to them on a temporary basis. After these women begin working, the Family Support Act will provide continued child care and medical insurance for up to one year.

JOBS offers basic education and skills training to AFDC mothers to enable them to get jobs. Child care is also made available to them. Each state handles its JOBS program slightly differently, but all were required to begin the project by October 1990. Some states allow women to remain on AFDC until their children are at least three years old without having to enroll in JOBS. Others require that they participate in a minimum number of training hours, even if they have younger children. Some states have special government-supported day-care centers; others reimburse parents for child care costs.

The Family Support Act also makes it easier for women on welfare to take action against husbands who neglect to pay child support. While passing bills in Congress is often an uphill battle, there is hope that future legislation will bring about more positive changes for all families.

Going It Alone

Not all women are single mothers because of divorce, a husband's death, or accidental pregnancy. Some women become single mothers by choice. They decide they want to raise a child by themselves. Maybe they haven't met "the right man," but they usually fear they are getting too old to postpone childbearing any longer. Others might never want to get married.

The number of single mothers by choice are still small, but in the 1980s the number of women over 30 who chose to have children by themselves increased by almost 70 percent from the previous decade. There are different methods available to women who wish to have children but remain single. Some chose to adopt, but the wait for a child can be long. Many women want the child to be their own. In that case, a woman can be impregnated by sperm from an anonymous donor or someone she knows. Usually the woman does not have sexual intercourse with the donor, but is artificially inseminated.

With all the problems that single mothers encounter, why would a woman intentionally take on the responsibility of raising a child by herself? It means she must be financially secure, emotionally stable, and able to provide child care. But the women who choose this role in life argue that a child who is truly wanted by a single mother is better off than one who is caught in the middle of an unhappy family. The choice of women to start a family by themselves would have been unheard of three decades ago. Today, independent women who want a family do not have to be married to have one. Says one woman contemplating just such a choice: "I could imagine going through life without a man, but I couldn't imagine going through life without a child." Today she no longer has to.

5 *High Tech Moms*

Until only recently, when a couple found out they were infertile, or unable to have children, their only option was to adopt a child. But once abortion became legal, there were fewer children to adopt. Some would-be parents became desperate to have a child.

In the past, infertility was often blamed on the woman. The Bible mentions two men, Abraham and Jacob, who were "disgraced" by infertile wives. Henry the Eighth, a King of England, took it a step further. When his wives were only able to produce female offspring, he beheaded them to marry yet another woman who might be able to give him a male heir to the throne. Today we know that it is actually the male who determines the sex of the baby, and that men are infertile just as often as women.

More couples have experienced difficulty conceiving children in recent years. There are many possible reasons for this. Women are delaying pregnancy until they are older, and older women often have a harder time getting pregnant. Prolonged use of birth control devices, venereal disease, and exposure to toxic chemicals in the environment can also cause infertility. The National Center for Health Statistics says there are about 3.5 million married couples in the United States who have not been able to have a baby. But today these people can find help for their problem in a number of ways.

Adoption

Adoption agencies are still one way that infertile couples and single people can become parents. These agencies are licensed by the state, and they carefully screen prospective parents to see if they are able to provide good homes for children who need them. Adoption can be a long process; instead of waiting nine months for a baby, adoptive parents often wait years. The wait is especially long if parents insist on adopting a white infant.

This single woman has adopted two children. Both boys were abandoned by their birth mothers.

Some agencies specialize in placing children who have suffered from abuse. When these children are taken from their birth parents, they are usually placed in foster homes for a while, then given to adoptive parents. Other agencies help place handicapped or seriously ill children. For example, many loving couples are taking babies with AIDS into their homes after their birth mothers have succumbed to the disease. Other families adopt foreign-born orphans. Children who were left without families after the 1989 Romanian revolution are being adopted by people in this country. After the Vietnam war, many Vietnamese children, from infancy to much older ages, were adopted by American couples.

Adoption through a state-licensed agency can take

years, and costs anywhere from $1,500 to $14,000. Some parents who are not willing to wait that long have taken a new route. In 44 states, independent adoptions are now legal. In this case, an agency doesn't handle the adoption. Instead, a third party—usually a lawyer, doctor, or clergyman—works with the birth mother and the adoptive parents to arrange the adoption. Independent adoptions cost anywhere from $6,200 to more than $18,000. This includes the birth mother's medical expenses and a fee paid to the third party who handles the legal aspects of the adoption. This kind of adoption has recently become more common because there are so few healthy, white babies available for adoption, and most people wanting to adopt are white.

Artificial Insemination

Until recently, adoption was the legal way for infertile couples to obtain a child. Today, science and technology have created a number of new ways for couples to have children. Of the 3.5 million couples who are infertile in the United States, 500,000 of them seek the new, nontraditional methods of conception now available. Sometimes infertility can be treated. It might be the result of a poor diet or fatigue, a condition where an individual's body is simply not functioning at full potential because of stress and other factors.

Male infertility is easier to diagnose than female infertility, so physicians generally begin testing the husband first. Doctors take a sperm sample for examination. If healthy sperm are present but in small quantities, pregnancy can be achieved by concentrating the sperm and *artificially inseminating* the wife. In this case, the child is genetically made from both parents.

If the husband is unable to produce sperm at all, the woman can be artificially inseminated with sperm from an anonymous donor, or perhaps from a friend or relative of the couple. Since the mother produces the egg, the child is, therefore, only genetically related

Louise Brown was the first "test-tube baby." She was born in England in 1979.

to the mother. This method is thus similar to adoption in many ways. It is often the method used by single women who make the decision to become pregnant without having a sexual relationship with a male.

In Vitro Fertilization

If a physician is certain that the husband is able to impregnate his wife, then the wife is tested. In the past, when a woman's body had certain physical problems that made childbearing difficult or impossible, a couple had to face the fact that they probably could never have children. Today, however, a number of new methods can treat women with problems relating to conception and childbearing.

Sometimes a woman's body does not ovulate, or produce and discharge an egg from the ovary during a woman's monthly cycle. When a woman ovulates, the egg is sent from one of the ovaries through the fallopian tubes and into the uterus. Sometimes the problem can be solved simply by taking drugs that help encourage the woman's body to ovulate. Then the couple can conceive normally. The use of fertility drugs has, however, often led to multiple births because more than one egg may be present in the uterus for fertilization by the father's sperm. Women who have used fertility drugs have a much higher incidence of having twins, triplets, or even as many as five or six children in one birth. This can be difficult for the woman physically and for the family financially.

Sometimes a doctor discovers that a woman's body produces eggs normally and that her uterus is capable of carrying a baby to term, but that the eggs are not making their way to the uterus. In this situation, a method called *in vitro fertilization* may be recommended. In this process the mother's egg is removed surgically from the ovary and is fertilized by her partner's sperm in a plastic laboratory petri dish. It is then placed in the woman's uterus where it develops just as it would in a traditional pregnancy. This is where the phrase "test tube baby" came from, even though a test-tube isn't actually used in the process.

In vitro fertilization is being performed at more and more clinics around the country, but it is very expensive. Families with only moderate incomes usually find it costs too much.

Like artificial insemination using the husband's sperm, *in vitro* fertilization produces a genetic child of both parents. If a woman's body does not produce eggs, she and her husband can have one or more donor eggs (from another female) fertilized *in vitro* by her husband's sperm and then implanted in the woman's uterus.

Older Mothers

Out of about 3.8 million births in 1987, 36,156 were to women over 40. This is an increase of more than 10,000—almost 30 percent from 10 years earlier. Some of these women were first-time mothers. Today, due to modern medical technology, women can have healthy babies later in life than ever before. *Obstetricians*, doctors who care for pregnant women and their babies, are telling women over age 40 who are in good health that there is no reason why they can't have children.

Often, getting pregnant is a common problem for older women who want children. But with the use of fertility drugs and *in vitro* fertilization, many older women today can have babies. While it is much easier for a woman to conceive after age 40 than it ever was before, a pregnancy later in life is still considered to be a high-risk pregnancy. These women may have complications from pregnancy such as diabetes, high blood pressure, and gall bladder problems, because their bodies are less able to take the stress of supporting two organisms. In addition, older women also have an increased rate of *miscarriage* (when the fetus is naturally aborted).

Doctors once worried that advanced age in pregnancy put the fetus at risk, but today's studies show that older women have little risk of premature or unhealthy babies. Older women do have a much higher risk, however, of bearing children with *Down syndrome*. A child with Down syndrome has moderate or severe mental deficiency and an abnormal physical appearance. At age 30, only 1 in 952 women will have children with Down syndrome. By age 40, the risk increases to 1 in 83. However, new technology now enables doctors to determine the health of the fetus before it is born. For women over 35, physicians strongly suggest use of this technology. One method is called *amniocentesis*. This procedure requires fluid from the mother's uterus which is obtained by inserting a hollow needle through the abdomen. Fluid in which the fetus' cells are floating is then studied to determine the sex of the fetus and to check for chromosomal abnormalities like Down syndrome. This test cannot be performed until the 16th week of pregnancy. A new test, called *chorionic villi sampling*, or CVS, can be performed even earlier to learn the same information. In this test, the doctor takes a sample of chorion, the membrane surrounding the fetal gestational sac. This sample can be studied in much the same way as the fluid from an amniocentesis.

Many doctors believe that increase in health consciousness has also made it safer for older women to bear children. "I think women today tend to be in better physical shape, and so in another five years, when researchers do another analysis of pregnancies, they won't even find as many complications as there are in the [studies] we are relying on now," says Dr. Manuel Alvarez of Mount Sinai School of Medicine.

Surrogate Mothers

A *surrogate mother* is a woman who carries a child to term for a couple who is unable to conceive. She is paid a fee to do so, usually about $10,000. The couple keeps the baby after the surrogate mother gives birth. In some cases, the woman may be carrying a child that used her own egg, and is therefore genetically her own. Some specialists estimate that there have been 4,000 such surrogate births since the 1970s.

Another form of surrogacy is called *gestational surrogacy*. In this case, even though a woman's body produces eggs, her uterus may not be able to carry a child. The couple's child will then be produced *in vitro* and placed in the surrogate's uterus. Usually these women sign contracts giving up all rights to the child.

Surrogacy has caused a number of legal and ethical problems. For one thing, many people are concerned that one day some women will no longer have to carry their own children if they choose not to. One can imagine a world, for example, where women will "rent" their uteri to women who do not want to be "inconvenienced" by pregnancy. The American Fertility Society and the American College of Obstetricians and Gynecologists are trying to limit surrogacy to cases of "medical need." Legislators around the country, particularly in California where surrogacy is more common, have considered laws restricting surrogacy. These bills are usually avoided, however, because of the emotional issues involved.

Many questions have arisen regarding surrogacy. Is a surrogate mother simply performing a service, even if the child is genetically half hers? Is she selling her baby? Does she have any right to a child that is either half hers or that she carried for nine months, even if she has signed a contract? One lawyer who has been involved in litigation for a surrogate mother says, "We've created a situation where we have more parents than we know what to do with." A researcher notes that allowing surrogate mothers to deny the contracts they signed will destroy the hopes of infertile couples who want a child. But if the contracts are binding, surrogacy may become a means of exploiting women.

In 1988, the well-known case of Baby M received national attention. Mary Beth Whitehead's egg was artificially inseminated by sperm from William Stern, because his wife was unable to conceive. The couple hoped that surrogacy would make it possible for them to become parents. Because the child was genetically 50 percent Whitehead's, she went to court after the birth of the baby to get custody of the child she had carried to term. She claimed to have "bonded" with the

Mary Beth Whitehead, left, is shown here with two fellow members of an organization that hopes to ban what they call the "slavery" of parenting for pay.

child—forming an emotional attachment so strong that she was unable to give it up. The Sterns eventually were awarded full custody of the child, whom they called Melissa. They did allow Whitehead to visit the girl—whom she calls Sara—as if the case had been a battle for custody after a divorce. The court did not rule in favor of the Sterns solely because of the contract; rather, they determined that they would provide a better home for the child. The legal issues surrounding the contract remain complicated.

A more recent California case involves a woman who was a gestational surrogate. Anna Johnson agreed to carry Mark and Crispina Calvert's child for a fee. Because Crispina's uterus could not carry a child, this method seemed the best alternative for them. It would still be their child genetically, but another woman would carry it to term. Says Mark Calvert, "We really wanted a child that had her [Crispina's] innocence, her sweetness, her demeanor."

Only one in 100 surrogacies end in legal action, and Johnson's is the first case where a gestational surrogate tried to get custody of the child she had carried—even though it was genetically no relation to her. But Johnson had signed a legal contract with the Calverts saying she would give them the child. The court awarded full custory to the Calverts, and none to Johnson. Although legal bills are still piling up, the Calverts are overjoyed to have Christopher Michael with them in their home. "All the sleepless nights, all the tears we've cried, financially, Christopher Michael's worth it," Mark Calvert says. They plan to tell their son about the special circumstances around his birth when he is old enough to understand. "He'll understand how much we loved him and how much we went through to have him," says Mark.

If surrogacy becomes more common, legislators will be forced to establish laws about this controversial birthing method. Contracts stating that the surrogate has no custodial rights to the child will have to be considered legal and binding, not something that can be disputed in court. But the question remains, will surrogacy become a legalized way to buy and sell babies? And will women who bear children become "baby-making machines," a title that seems to go against every goal of the feminist movement?

Modern Mothers

There are many new issues surrounding motherhood and parenting in today's society. It seems much more difficult than it was when women had fewer choices, when infertile couples had no medical alternatives to turn to, and when women were expected to stay home to care for their children. As the world becomes more technologically advanced and our attitudes about women continue to change, there is no doubt that the concept and definition of motherhood will follow suit.

Who's to say whether all this change will be good? With more and more women joining the work force, financial independence will result in longer days in the workplace and less time at home. Single mothers will continue to face hardships while trying to raise children by themselves. And surrogacy and other fertility issues are so different from anything currently on the law books that legislators and parents have little idea how to cope with them.

As our world continues to change, however, one thing is certain: New laws and assistance to women will have to accompany change. Women who work will need more options. Single mothers will need more help getting back on their feet. Mothers who choose to stay home when their children are young should have the opportunity to go back to work once their children are in school. Surrogate mothers, children born of surrogate mothers, and the parents of these children will all need legal protection. Hopefully, the '90s will be the decade when world legislators and business leaders catch up to the changes that women have experienced during the last 30 years.

Glossary

AID TO FAMILIES WITH DEPENDENT CHILDREN (AFDC). Government assistance provided to parents with children who are unable to work to support their families.

ALIMONY. Financial support given to a woman by her ex-husband after they have divorced.

AMNIOCENTESIS. A medical procedure that can check the health and determine the sex of the fetus. A hollow needle is inserted into the woman's abdominal wall and then into the uterus. Fluid is taken from the uterus. In the fluid are cells from the fetus that can be studied to analyze the number of chromosomes in the fetus. If there is an extra chromosome 21 (a specific chromosome), the child has Down syndrome. If it has two of chromosome X, it is female. If it has only one chromosome X and one chromosome Y, it is male.

ARTIFICIAL INSEMINATION. A medical method that combines a man's sperm with a woman's egg outside of the body.

AU PAIR. A person, usually a young girl from a foreign country, hired to care for a family's children. She usually receives a small salary and room and board.

BABY BOOM. The era between the years of 1946 and 1964 when the birth rate increased greatly in the United States.

CHILD SUPPORT. Financial support paid to a man's

children after he and his ex-wife have divorced.

CHORIONIC VILLI SAMPLING (CVS). A test where the doctor takes a sample of chorion, the membrane surrounding the fetal gestational sac. This sample can be studied in much the same way as the fluid from an amniocentesis test to discover the same results.

DOWN SYNDROME. An abnormality that results in mental deficiency and abnormal physical appearance of a baby.

EQUAL RIGHTS AMENDMENT (ERA). An amendment proposed by Congress that stated "Equality of rights under the law shall not be denied or abridged by the United States or by any State on account of sex." In 1982, the amendment did not pass when too few states chose to ratify it.

FAMILY SUPPORT ACT. A 1988 law that helps AFDC recipients learn to support themselves. Under this act, the Job Opportunities and Basic Skills (JOBS) program provides job training and child care to mothers so they can enter the work force.

FAMILY WAGE. The popular attitude in mid-20th-century America that male workers should be paid enough money to support their families so their wives did not have to work.

FEMINISM. The theory that women should have the same social, economic and sexual rights as men.

GESTATIONAL SURROGACY. A type of surrogate motherhood where the woman carries a baby to term that is not genetically her own.

IN VITRO. A process where a mother's egg is fertilized

by her partner's sperm in a plastic laboratory dish. The egg is then implanted in the woman's (or a surrogate's) uterus where it develops just as it would in a traditional pregnancy.

MATERNITY LEAVE, PARENTAL LEAVE. A temporary leave of absence taken by a parent, usually the mother, after birth. Many countries, particularly in Europe, require employers to give women a specific amount of time after childbirth to care for their infant. Although the United States has tried to pass such a bill, it has yet to become a law.

MISCARRIAGE. An occurrence where a fetus is naturally aborted by a woman's body.

MOMMY TRACK. A term used to describe the faltering careers of many working mothers who had to devote less time to their careers because they chose to have children.

NANNY. A professionally trained woman who cares for a family's children.

OBSTETRICIANS. Doctors who care for pregnant women and their babies.

SUFFRAGETTES. Women in the United States who worked for their right to vote. The suffragettes were an organized effort from 1860 to 1920.

SURROGATE MOTHERS. Women who carry a fetus to term for infertile couples. Sometimes the baby is genetically the couple's and the process is called *gestational* surrogacy; the surrogate mother acts only as a "living incubator." Other times, the baby is genetically 50 percent the surrogate's.

Bibliography

Books

Genevie, Louis and Eva Margolies. *The Motherhood Report*. New York: MacMillan Publishing Company, 1986.

Glotzbach, Gerri. *Adoption*. Vero Beach, Florida: The Rourke Corporation, Inc., 1990.

Periodicals

Angier, Natalie. "Baby Chic." *Mademoiselle*, June 1989: 194.

Berg, Elizabeth. "Why I'm At Home." *Parents*, April 1987.

Darnton, Nina. "Mommy Vs. Mommy." *Newsweek*, June 4, 1990: 64.

Elmer-Dewitt, Philip. "The Great Experiment." *Time*, Special Issue: Fall 1990: 72.

Garis, Leslie. "Staying Home in the '80s." *Vogue*, April , 1987.

Gaylin, Jody. "What Do You Do?" *Parents*, November 1988: 127.

Gibbs, Nancy. "The Dreams of Youth." *Time*, Special Issue: Fall 1990: 10.

Groller, Ingrid. "Women and Work." *Parents*, July 1990: 64.

Gress-Wright, Jessica. "ABC and Me." *Commentary*, January 1990: 29.

Harris, Lisa C. "Different Kinds of Mothering." *Parents*, July, 1987: 59.

Hudson, Gail E. "Home Full Time and Loving It." *Parents*, May 1990: 80.

Kasindorf, Jeanie. "Mommy Oldest." *New York*, July 17, 1989: 23.

Kreyche, Gerald F. "Surrogate Motherhood: An Ethical and Moral Dilemma." *USA Today*, November 1987: 66.

Parsons, Dana. "A Six-Pack Toast to the Kinder and Gentler Pete Wilson." *Los Angeles Times*, January 13, 1991: B1.

Prose, Francine. "Living With Choices." *Parents*, May 1989: 131.

Smith, Marguerite T. "Fighting To Have It All." *Money*, January 1990: 130.

Smolowe, Jill. "Last Call For Motherhood." *Time*, Special Issue: Fall 1990: 76.

Stern, Zev. "Surrogate Motherhood and Medical Alternatives for Childless Couples." *USA Today*, November 1987: 70.

Turner, Jason, Gina Barbaro, and Myles Schlank. "Head Start and JOBS: Collaborative Efforts Help Families Become Self-Sufficient." *Children Today*, May-June 1990: 12.

Weller, Sheila. "One Woman's Family: The Plight of Single Mothers." *McCall's*, February, 1989: 75.

Woodman, Sue. "Mid-life Miracle: A First Baby at 40." *Women's Day*, July 10, 1990: 66.

Index

About The Author

Elizabeth Sirimarco has written three other books for young people. She is also the editor of the *Women Today* series, of which this book is a part. A graduate of the University of Colorado, Elizabeth now lives in Laguna Beach, California.

Picture Credits

AP Wide World Photos: 8, 20, 48, 50, 55
Christie Costanzo: 11
The Image Works: 4 (Patsy Davidson); 17 (Annie Hunter); 26 (Carl Glassman); 28 (Elizabeth Crews); 30 (Howard Dratch); 36 (David Strickler); 38 (Shelley Gazin); 46 (John Griffin)
Photo Researchers, Inc.: 14 (Shirley Zeiberg); 24 (Leonard Lessin); 32 (Ed Lettau); 42 (Ulrike Welsch)

Franklin Pierce College Library

00039174